Mercury

by J.P. Bloom

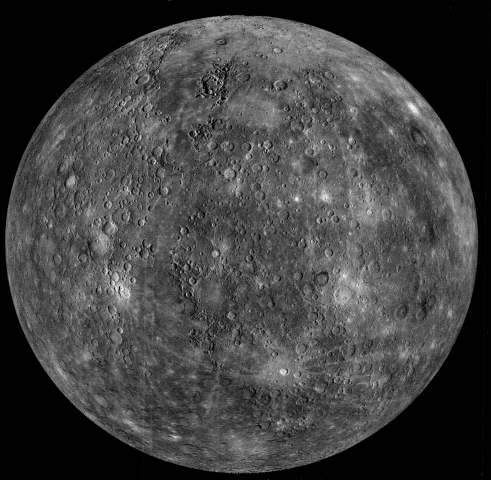

ABDO

PLANETS

Kids

abdopublishing.com

Published by Abdo Kids, a division of ABDO, PO Box 398166, Minneapolis, Minnesota 55439.

Printed in the United States of America, North Mankato, Minnesota.

102014
012015

THIS BOOK CONTAINS RECYCLED MATERIALS

Photo Credits: NASA, Science Source, Shutterstock, Thinkstock
Production Contributors: Teddy Borth, Jennie Forsberg, Grace Hansen
Design Contributors: Candice Keimig, Laura Rask, Dorothy Toth

Library of Congress Control Number: 2014943795
Cataloging-in-Publication Data
J.P. Bloom.
 Mercury / J.P. Bloom.
  p. cm. -- (Planets)
ISBN 978-1-62970-718-1 (lib. bdg.)
Includes index.
1. Mercury (Planet)--Juvenile literature. 2. Solar system--Juvenile literature. I. Title.
523.41--dc23
                    2014943795

Table of Contents

Mercury

Mercury is a **planet**. Planets **orbit** stars. Planets in our solar system orbit the sun.

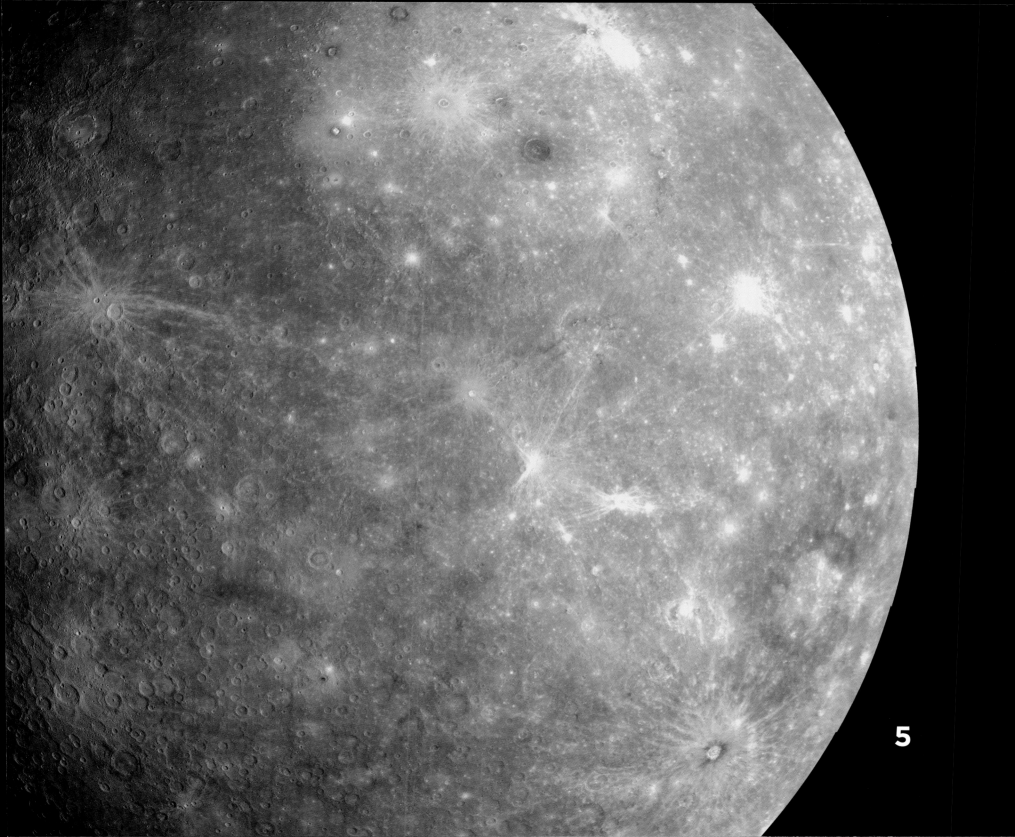

5

Mercury is the closest **planet** to the sun. It is about 36 million miles (58 million km) from the sun.

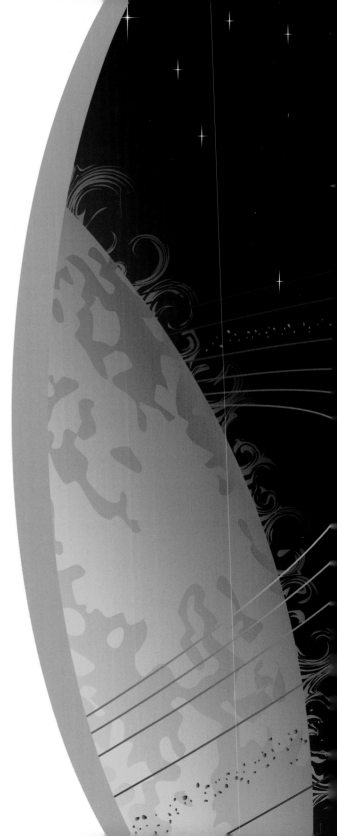

Venus

Mars

Saturn

Neptune

Uranus

Jupiter

Earth

Mercury

Mercury **orbits** the sun every 88 days. One year on Mercury is 88 days on Earth.

Sun

Mercury

9

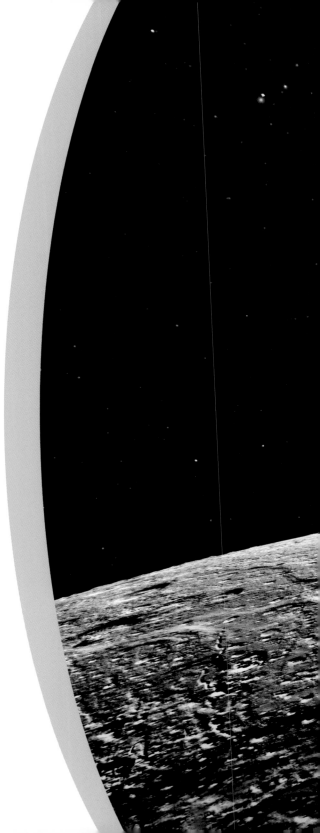

Mercury spins while it **orbits**

the sun. It spins very slowly.

10

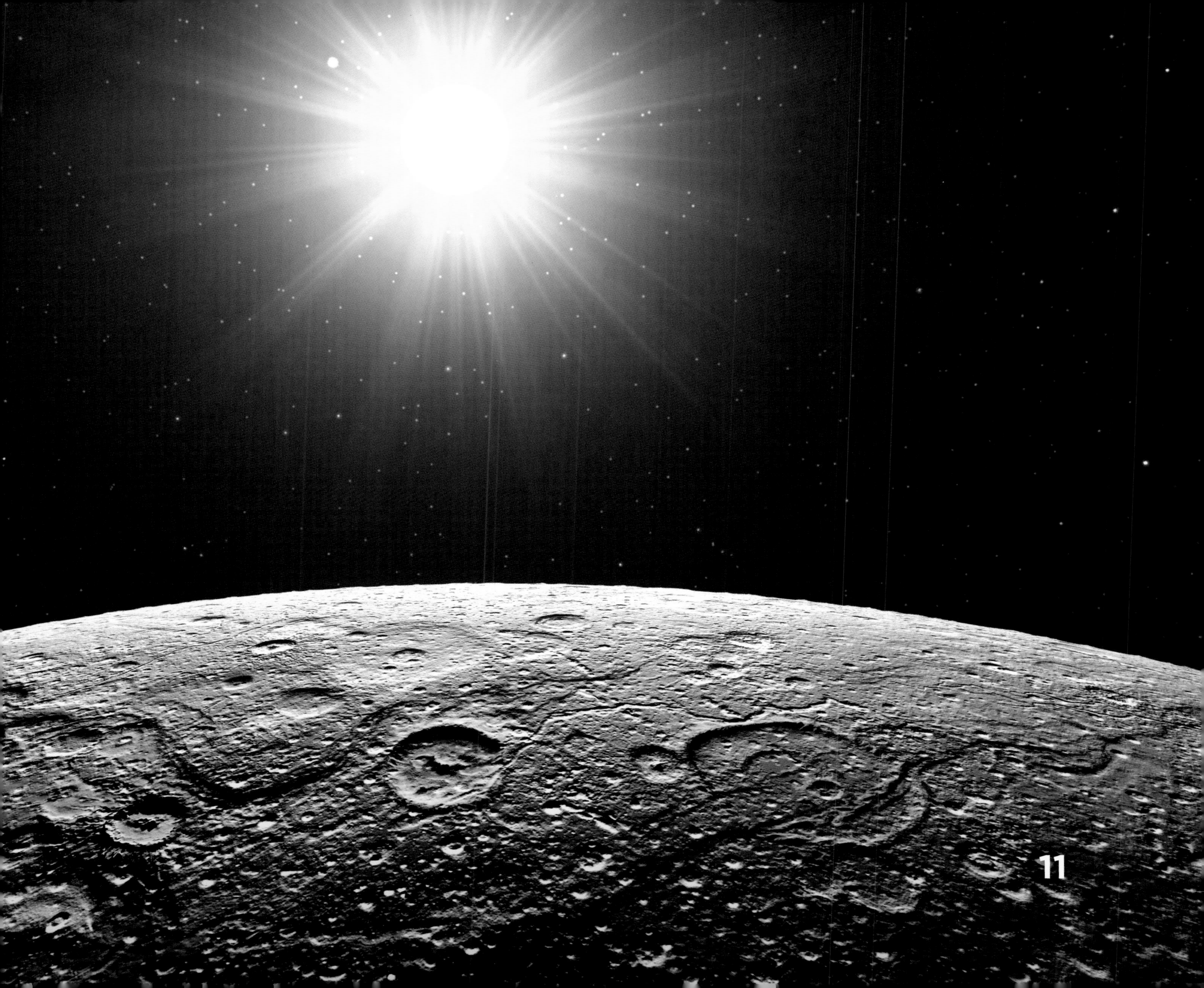

The spin makes day and night. One day on Mercury is 59 days on Earth.

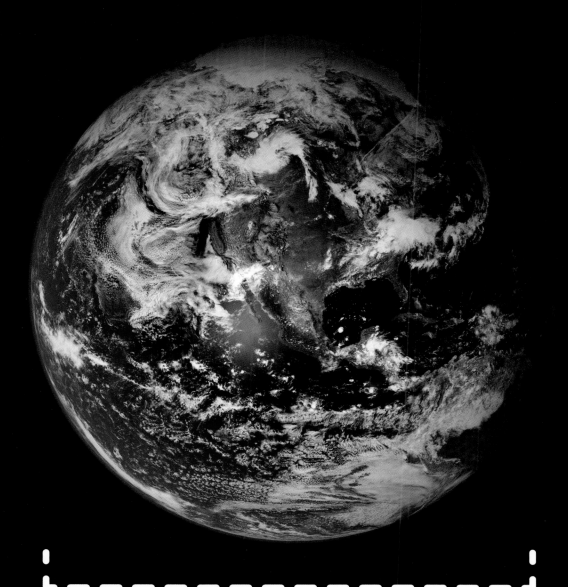

**Mercury
3,032 miles
(4,879 km)**

Earth 7,918 miles (12,742 km)

Mercury has three layers.

It has a core, mantle, and

crust. Its core is made of iron.

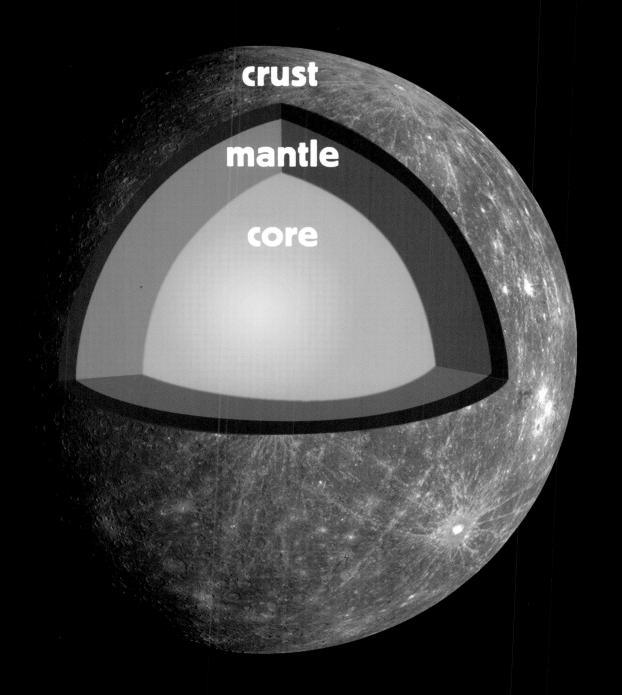

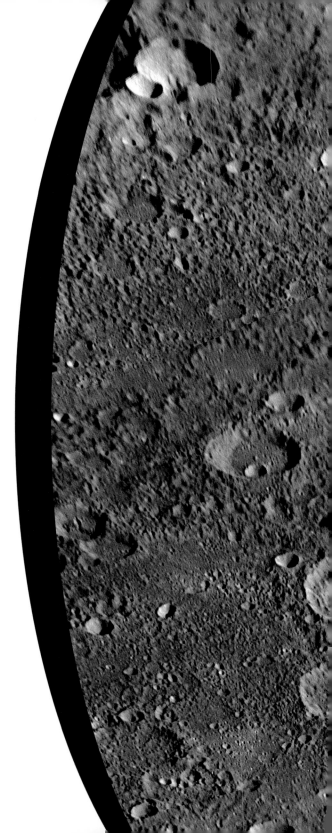

Mercury's **terrain** is rough.

It is covered in large **craters**.

16

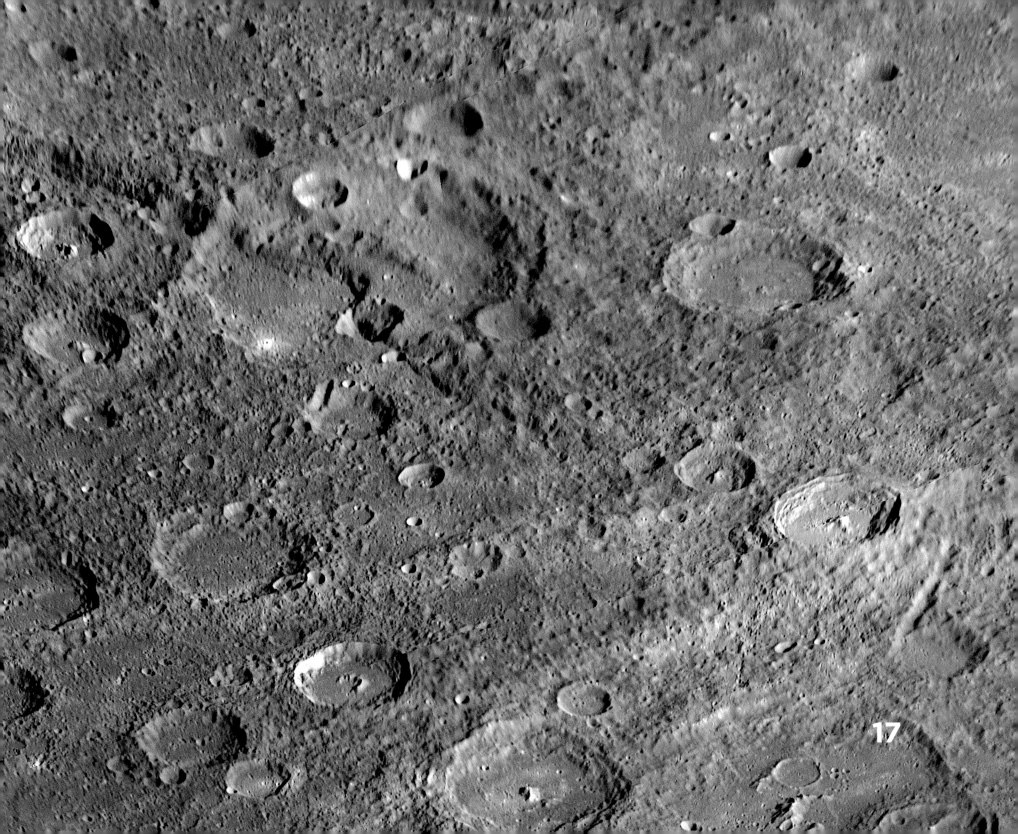

Hot and Cold

Mercury can be very hot or cold. Humans and animals cannot live there. Plants cannot live there either.

day
up to 800° F
(427° C)

night
down to -280° F
(-173° C)

19

Mercury from Earth

You can see Mercury from Earth. You can see it without a telescope.

----- **Mercury**

More Facts

- Mercury once had **craters** that were filled with magma. When the magma cooled, it created a surface similar to Earth's moon's surface.

- Mercury's temperature ranges from -280 degrees F to 800 degrees F (-173° C to 427° C).

- Mercury is the fastest planet to orbit the sun. It is named after the Roman god Mercury, who was said to be the speediest of the gods.

Glossary

crater – a dip in the ground shaped like a large bowl.

orbit – the path of a space object as it moves around another space object. To orbit is to follow this path.

planet – a large, round object in space (such as Earth) that travels around a star (such as the sun).

terrain – the physical features of an area of land. Mountains, rivers, and canyons can all be part of a terrain.

Index

abdokids.com

Use this code to log on to abdokids.com and access crafts, games, videos, and more!

Abdo Kids Code:
PMK7181